REFUGEES

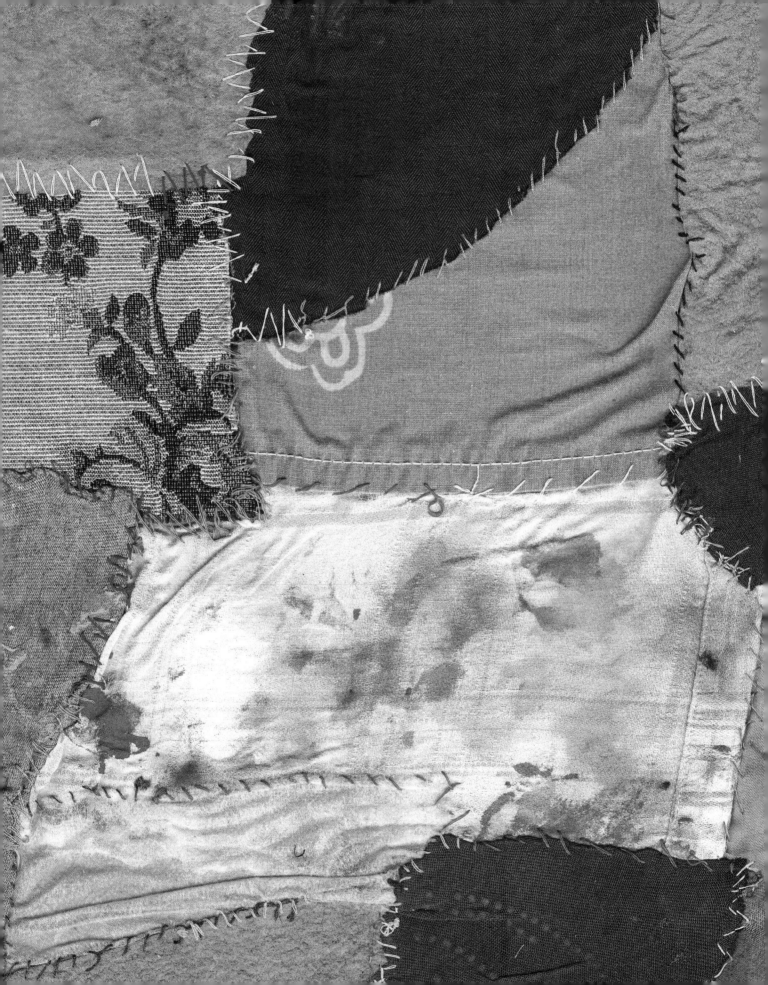

To bridges –

and those who have need to cross them B.B.

For all beings who must overcome intolerance

to find their home J.S.

With special thanks to Delvy Betancourt for her collaboration
with the coloured backgrounds

Refugees copyright © Palazzo Editions Limited 2019
Text copyright © Brian Bilston 2019
Illustrations copyright © Jose Sanabria 2019

First published in Great Britain in 2019 by
Palazzo Editions Limited, 15 Church Road, London SW13 9HE
www.palazzoeditions.com
This paperback edition published in 2022

Editor: Gemma Farr
Designer: Arianna Osti

A CIP catalogue record for this book is available from the British Library.

ISBN: 978-1-78675-129-4

Printed and bound in Dubai

BRIAN BILSTON

REFUGEES

Illustrated by
JOSÉ SANABRIA

PALAZZO

They have no need of our help

So do not tell me

These haggard faces could belong to you or me

Should life have dealt a different hand

We need to see them for who they really are
Chancers and scroungers
Layabouts and loungers
With bombs up their sleeves
Cut-throats and thieves

They are not
Welcome here
We should make them
Go back to where they came from

They cannot
Share our food
Share our homes
Share our countries
Instead let us
Build a wall to keep them out

It is not okay to say
These are people just like us
A place should only belong to those who are born there

Do not be so stupid to think that
The world can be looked at another way.

The world can be looked at another way
Do not be so stupid to think that
A place should only belong to those who are born there
These are people just like us

It is not okay to say
Build a wall to keep them out
Instead let us
Share our countries
Share our homes
Share our food

They cannot
Go back to where they came from
We should make them
Welcome here

They are not
Cut-throats and thieves
With bombs up their sleeves
Layabouts and loungers
Chancers and scroungers

We need to see them for who they really are
Should life have dealt a different hand
These haggard faces could belong to you or me

So do not tell me
They have no need of our help

REFUGEES

By Brian Bilston

They have no need of our help
So do not tell me
These haggard faces could belong to you or me
Should life have dealt a different hand
We need to see them for who they really are
Chancers and scroungers
Layabouts and loungers
With bombs up their sleeves
Cut-throats and thieves
They are not
Welcome here
We should make them
Go back to where they came from
They cannot
Share our food
Share our homes
Share our countries
Instead let us
Build a wall to keep them out
It is not okay to say
These are people just like us
A place should only belong to those who are born there
Do not be so stupid to think that
The world can be looked at another way

(Now read from bottom to top)